# Paco's Pet

**Damian Harvey**
**Illustrated by Mike Brownlow**

OXFORD

ZOO

Tickets

Can I have a pet?

No you can not.

Can I have that as a pet?

No you can not.

Can I have this as a pet?

No!
Put it back.

Can I have that as a pet?

No!
Put it down.

Can I have this as a pet?

No!
Get down.

Can I have ...

... lots of pets?
NO!

# Feed the animals

15

# Find out more ...

Read about Ant's pet hamster ...

Shoo Rayner    OXFORD    Jon Stuart

A Dog's Day

OXFORD    Claire Llewellyn

... or Cat's day with Pip the dog.